What's Happening in the Shade

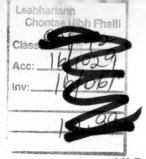

First published in 2015 by
Liberties Press
140 Terenure Road North | Terenure | Dublin 6W
T: +353 (1) 905 6072|E: info@libertiespress.com | W: libertiespress.com

Trade enquiries to Gill & Macmillan Distribution
Hume Avenue | Park West | Dublin 12
T: +353 (1) 500 9534 | F: +353 (1) 500 9595 | E: sales@gillmacmillan.ie

Distributed in the United Kingdom by
Turnaround Publisher Services
Unit 3 | Olympia Trading Estate | Coburg Road | London N22 6TZ
T: +44 (0) 20 8829 3000 | E: orders@turnaround-uk.com

Distributed in the United States by
Casemate-IPM | 22841 Quicksilver Dr | Dulles, VA 20166
T: +1 (703) 661-1586 | F: +1 (703) 661-1547 | E: ipmmail@presswarehouse.com

ISBN: 978-1-909718-96-8
2 4 6 8 10 9 7 5 3 1

A CIP record for this title is available from the British Library.

Cover design by Karen Vaughan – Liberties Press
Internal design by Liberties Press

What's Happening
in the Shade

Liam Ryan

Gillian
Orlaith
Sarah

Contents

Acknowledgements

Acknowledgements are due to the editors of the following, where some of these poems, or versions of them, were previously published.

Poetry Ireland Review: 'The Meadow'

The Shop: 'The Pin',
'The Man from Porlock'

Cyphers: 'Knowledge' from
'Gnostic Psalms',
'Over in Japan'

The Moth: 'Undiminished'

Revival: 'The New Bar',
'Occupational Therapy'

Southword: 'Evening',
'Breakfast in London',
'Preparation for Battle'

Ten Years in the Doghouse: 'Sunday Night in
Golden', 'Blueprints'

Outburst: 'Invitation', 'Report',
'Of Poetry'

'The New Bar' won third prize at Strokestown International Poetry Festival 2012.

'Curriculum Vitae' won third prize at Galway University Hospital Trust Poetry Competition 2013.

'Orpheus' won third prize in The Francis Ledwidge International Poetry Competition 2014.

'The Pin' appeared in the anthology *fathers and what must be said*, Rebel Poetry, 2014.

The support of Hugh O'Donnell, Noel King and Thomas McCarthy is greatly appreciated.

I

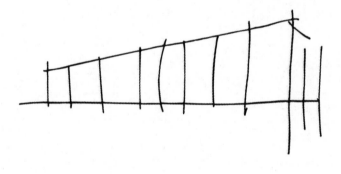

Of Poetry

The sun crouching low
angled a pane of burnt light;

the train gathering speed
slung a full bucket of sound;

a sheet flapping and slapping
caught a full sail of wind;

nervous mouseleaves
scurried across the road;

the pigeon's singular applause
its clapped-out routine;

a cloud of skittish starlings
blackened out the whole field;

the sea coming and going
frothed its hems on the sand;

her face in the rearview mirror
wore a blindfold of light;

the goosepimple rash
sprinkled across the nightsky;

the calfwords kicking their heels,
bouncing in the abundant fields.

The New Bar

Some years later when they were fitting
a new bar in the lounge I was called in
to consult with the fire officer about
relocating one of the exit doors.
He was a small contrary little man
with a well-thumbed copy of the Building
Regulations, terrified of making a decision.
I could talk to him, tease him about footballers
and some sense seemed to alight in his head.
The double doors out onto the Square were open,
the new bar had just arrived from the joiners'
workshop, its incense of resin and glue
filled the strange emptiness of the space;
the voices echoing, bouncing around the room.

While they were stuck on some boring detail
with the electrician about alarms and signs,
the interior designer arrived with her samples,
the builder stood up, straightening his back
and I wandered over to the spot inside the door
where I had fallen in love with you
that Friday night after a book launch.
You standing, yapping, radiant and wild,
tearing into someone about, was it, politics,
and of course revelling in my attention.
But there wasn't a sign of it left there,
the wallpaper steamed off, the carpets gone,
floorboards lifted for new wires and pipes,
even the very tiles you stood on, gone.

The Inviolability of Geometry

1. Woodturning

You create by cutting away;
crouched over the lathe
in your little workshop,
eyes straining behind goggles,
sawdust clogging your hair,
chippings softening the floor,
cobwebs a hessian of dust,
bits and chisels on the bench.

You can read in the blocks
of wood stacked to dry
the fruit bowl and lampshade;
you can feel them in your hands,
sanded, polished, crafted;
you can see the light picking out
the fine pen-and-ink lines of
the spalted beech's signature.

2. Mathematics

It was always tempting
to take refuge in
the inviolability of geometry;
its refined lines angled

with such definite precision;
triangles tall and lean or
squatting with solid intent;
or in the faithfulness of numbers,
their accountability always
adding up to something.
But ultimately they stood naked,
an array of rafters pristine
in the proud light of evening,
waiting on the felt and slates.

Inspections during Construction

The jackhammer
steel-pecking the road,
bringing in the water;

a red-eyed laser
beeping at the staff,
setting the level straight;

the radon barrier
lapped and taped,
sealing out the earth;

the fair-faced blockwork,
buckets of scud,
a plasterer on stilts;

the cills sitting proud,
a cold bridge
at their backs;

joists taking
bilateral tension
between the wallplates;

the rafter's snug fit,
the purlins' backbone,
carrying up the roof;

the morse-code tapping
of slating nails
between the showers;

solar panels,
trapping the sun
in a tank of water;

cleanline windows
with u-values
touching the floor;

Indian granite last
into the kitchen,
finishing off the island;

the sunroom's view,
the rain-rinsed sky,
flimsy filigree of light;

the en-suite tiled out,
a painter touching up,
your face in the mirror;

the carpet's footprints,
the strange bed
where you will be waked;

the entrance splayed open,
kerbs holding back the lawn,
the daffodil's final touch.

The Blockie

Somehow we'd managed to miss
each other for a good few years.
He wasn't on the sites I visited;
he worked the south of the county
and anyhow I seem to recall
he preferred the smaller jobs,
extensions for people he knew,
and the occasional house.
Lately I'd heard he'd retired.

This morning at the shop,
I recognised the stooped walk,
the same loose cardigan,
the solid build of someone
who walked dodgy scaffoldings
scooping mortar off a lid,
lifting concrete blocks,
tamping them plumb
with the heel of his trowel.

A newspaper under his arm
as if ready for the tea-break banter,
he hobbled on an arthritic hip,
slowly eased out into traffic.
His weathered face now pale,
the loose flesh corpsing;
the scaffolds of work removed,
fumbling towards old age,
fear settling in his eyes.

Ancillary Notes to a Pre-Purchase Report

The wicket gate bursting with rust;
the girlish faces of new daffodils
dying to make the May altar;
kerbs struggling to restrain
the spreading paunch of moss-lawn;
brambles, those cheeky trespassers,
streeling nonchalantly around corners.
The roughened surface of concrete
ramped up at the back door;
the garden hose all reeled in,
a shovel and a sledgehammer
stood down in the garden shed,
a radio frozen, leaking its batteries;
last year's onions hanging from a nail.

Cobwebs lurked along the cornices;
windows of sun-worn carpet shadowed
the sitting-room floor; graduate photographs
highlighted squares of floral wallpaper;
kitchen chairs with their backs up were
kneeling against a table; duvets coverless,
slack and cold, laid out across the bed;
a commode pretending to be a chair,
a large-digit telephone no one dialled,
long-winged taps stuck in the kitchen sink,
a cistern leaking, a purlin sagging,
moisture ingress under the flashings;
a consultant's card with the last appointment
stuck on the calendar's month of death.

A Design Brief for a Funeral Parlour

The first point of contact, the office,
to have a decent hardwood door;
wainscoting along the party wall;
large rooflights in sloping ceiling,
a bit of carpet on the floor, room
for a table, a few chairs, a filing cabinet;
easy access to the store shelved
out for about three dozen coffins,
more than enough choice for
this small town in county Laois.

A reposing room, no great need
for windows here, allow mourners
ease of movement in and out,
a large overhanging canopy at the front
ideal for a removals of wet evenings.
And somewhere at the back, out of sight,
space for an embalming room, small,
about three metres by two wide,
a plastic table with channels at the side,
shelving for all the bottles of liquid,
a suction-type pipe, a toilet-
like discharge plumbed to the sewer;
and a mechanical hoist with ratchets,
steel wire for the dead weight.

The Barbarians

after Cavafy

We were so well prepared,

with priests and curates
in every little parish;

reformatories to house
the delinquent kids;

laundries to take in
the fallen girls;

convents of nuns
with sisters of mercy.

We were so well prepared
to fight the barbarians.

We had managers banking
in pinstripe suits;

flood plains rezoned
under a deluge of representations;

builders stacking up
shares in bloodstock;

jeeps at the ready
in every tarmaced driveway.

We were so well prepared.

Yet Another Business Seminar

Here they come, the guys in shiny shoes,
in well-cut suits with short back and sides,
laptops slung over their shoulders,
striding through the foyer with smartphones bleeping;
here are the guys who know the jargon,
the BS numbers, the statutory instruments.
These are the guys from sales and marketing,
the managers, bankers, company directors,
familiar with the trappings of the small print,
upwardly mobile or down on their luck.
These are the guys on the corporate ladder,
taking their chances, doing the business.

These are the guys with mileage allowances,
with crisp cuffs and neat wedding bands;
these are the guys who trawled online
and caught you in those fishnet tights;
these are the guys striding across the
Liffey bridge for their half-hour appointment;
these are the guys who'll never know your name,
nor care less if you are Italian or Brazilian;
these are the guys taking their pound of flesh,
paying their way, sealing the deal.
These are the guys on the corporate ladder,
taking their chances, doing the business.

The Lie of the Land

I
A convoy of lorries turning at Kellys'
crushed the morning with crunching tyres
before tearing along the narrow lane with
twenty tons of the finest gravel;
leaves hung naked in talcumed dust.

Topsoil pushed, peeled back,
the earth opened, gaped, raw,
purloined, pillaged and plundered;
the mechanical shovel prowling, growling,
dumping gravel onto steel screens.

A container housing office and toilet
stranded on a left over patch of grass;
the Wavin pipe running to ground;
the quarry creeping across the field;
an absence growing to a desolate yawn.

II
zoning maps
discussed in every
pub in town

the architect with village
proposals aping
El Forum in Barcelona

the new theodolite
bought in for the
topographical survey

the real estate agent
with glossy brochures
and new smartphone

the bank manager
moved sideways for
being prudent with money

the stretch limousine
heading up to Punchestown
of an ordinary Thursday

the aging solicitor
almost hidden behind
piles of conveyancing files

the visual-only
inspections from
the rolled-down window

the stage payments
approved, closing
documentation to follow

the magnum of champagne
popping in the pub
sealing the deal

III
steel palisade
ring-fencing
fields of thistles

timber-frame skeletons
blue felt flapping
red clots of fire-stopping

shop windows vacant,
pub doors locked,
not even a For Sale sign

queues out the door
of the post office
every Friday morning

phone calls from
bank managers
on Friday evenings

NAMA and liquidators
receivers and split mortgages
on the tip of our tongues

fire sale auctions
attracting cash buyers
for vacant possession

the joiner on Skype
from Calgary with
his Canadian girlfriend

the carpenter in Perth or
Melbourne moving
in with his Aussie partner

the fathers at Dublin
airport on Sunday evenings
heading to London, or Sweden.

IV
Wisps of grass are now stealing back;
evening light pours nonchalantly
along the exposed banks of gravel;
an occasional hare sits, looks,
then lopes away with its lazy stride.

The screen now lopsided, angled,
rusting; oil drums, yellow and blue,
fallen over dead in their black vomit;
the remains of an old Anglia car,
love-seats gone, bonnet gaping.

The veined walls; layered grey;
the roughly cobbled floor sunk,
courting danger on the water table.
Pools blinking on the terrain map;
puddles, lost coins of light.

Catching the Wisps

There is so much to admire.

Day and night spooned together,
their only child's carefree mooning
reflecting them in a cold light;

the daffodil's head, cheeky, inquisitive,
peeking through winter's blanket of clay,
its tubes of yellow well hidden;

the pair of lime trees with truck-
stopping trunks all doused in perfume
for one single week every year;

the indecisiveness of water gulping
down streams, only to sit pretty
in still pools guarding fish.

And so much to miss too.

How every morning day bullies night,
brushes it aside like a foggy dream
or an old-fashioned pang of conscience;

how moisture, if given half a chance,
will infiltrate old convent walls
to flare vibrant mushroom rot,

how the sycamore with arms full of crows'
nests and spineless ivy, goes wild
with the wind and wrecks the cottage roof;

how the fridge-freezer late at night
jolts from sleep and with lilting lisps
resuscitates its slow dance with the daffodils.

And will you have seen time laid out
in long swathes sweltering in the meadow,
how every single one was raked in,
piked up neatly with weary arms,

and will you have seen the float,
low to the ground, steel-trimmed tail,
bearing the pikes up the road, home;
the bushes doing their business, catching the wisps.

What Are You to Do

I
There has always been something
about the way windows of light
wash across the floorboards,
lie nonchalantly against
the metal stove, listening
to its flue tediously tuning
to the vagaries of the sky,
whilst the out-of-focus
twigs shimmer and dance
along the kitchen wall.

II
What are you to do of a cold
dark evening in late November
when you see sitting on a hedge
dribbling, drooling with dew,
dithering like a weak balloon,
the huge face of the moon
languidly liquidly lifting
itself up out of the cold field?

Soaked, saturated, festooned,
its casual, cowed cowface,
a huge hubcap mirror
masking its lunar vacancy,
the gleaming gloated face
stalling me to a full stop,
pulling a massive tidal wave
surging through my heart.

Undiminished

I love the way a hedgerow or stand of trees
stops short right in the middle of a field,
as if the architect of lands had daringly decided
to abandon his line nowhere in all that space.
This January evening it just stands there
like a line of spectators on a terrace,
up to its ankles in the soggy grass,
a few seagulls a long way inland,
a waterhen scurrying for shelter,
no sign of a bullock or heifer anywhere,
too early for the shy snowdrops
or the dollops of primrose colour.
Just the evening sun spilling out
across the sky behind Raheen chapel,
the first tentative cocksteps
giving birth to another year,
while unfettered by Land Commission divides,
unencumbered by posts and wire,
stands this calm, unembarrassed witness,
its knowledge of hayseed undiminished.

Evening

I
The day is signed off
with the forward slash
of a disinterested moon,
its shy diminutive flourish
sits askance the southern sky,
its nail-clipping of light,
a rent in the tent of dark;

unaware, unperturbed
by our damp darkness,
it indifferently slides
behind the closing clouds,
turning its back on us,
its blade-face to the sun,
a fragile ligature of light.

II
after Paul Celan

Blackmilk of daybreak
played his lifelong fugue;
they were already digging
a grave in the evening sky.

Hope, as dry as almonds,
never enough to live by,
shoals being trawled away
under a mackerel sky.

He chiselled out
blackened words
as freight trains trundled
under a darkening sky.

A chorus of crows,
a calling calligraphy,
all skyping together
against the hare's pelt sky.

Marine

I
after Paul Verlaine

Slumbering seas breathe,
swell deeply, even swoon
beneath the plangent
face of the love-lost moon.

The harsh chirography
of light's signature
earths the looming sky,
feigning widespread torture.

Rocks are smothered,
worn out in the crash
of the sea's ebullient
mating crush.

The cathedral skies
are ripped, burst apart,
the resounding, pounding,
thunderous harmless fart.

II
after Arthur Rimbaud

Rearing up in feverish madness,
currents race urgently, aimlessly,
splashing light, burnished and burnt,

sparks spraying off forged steel,
anvil lashing, blasting, crashing.

While the ebb-tide glides,
coasts effortlessly into the harbour,
muffling, hugging the stranded rocks,
courting, lapping the stilts of the pier,
caressing, blessing with whirls of light.

Snap Shots

I
Leuigh 1967
Molly Slattery,
all in black
looking out
over her gate.

II
Foildearg
Two goats, spancelled,
one stooping, pissing,
of a wet evening,
above Leuigh.

III
Lisheen
The little stoup
inside the door;
his two fingers,
dripping wet.

IV
Lisheen
The scythe standing,
its curlew blade
dipping to his stone,
whetting its edge.

V
Topless
She was standing
at the kitchen window,
washing herself,
topless.

VI
Near Clonoulty
A rabbit sitting
behind a hedge
watching match traffic
burst blisters of tar.

VII
Passing
The house bursting,
light leaking
out through
the door bell.

VIII
Waiting
I could have drunk
coffee all day
just to sit there
admiring her bum.

IX
Intent
The first thing
she did was stop
at the petrol station
to buy condoms.

X
Red Carpet
Without fail
the women
are mounted
on high heels.

XI
In Love
My chest heaving
against the treachery
of breaths
without you.

XII
Croke Park
Seagulls swirling
in over the stadium,
ignoring the
roars of the crowd.

XIII
Las Palmas
Under my window
the empty retching
of the sea throwing
up on the sand.

XIV
Woodstown Strand
With purls and crossply
the rivulet stitched

an Aran sleeve
in the sand.

XV
Bunker Shot
Shoes shuffling,
nestling into the sand,
salmon spawning
in the riverbed.

XVI
Gnostic Golfer
The knowledge
of sweet contact
in the palms
of my hands.

XVII
Time
The rope slipping,
cutting welts
of pain caulking
to calluses of grief

XVIII
Days
The days, like
disinterested kittens,
are stepping
away from me.

XIX
Dirt
A few shovelfuls
of dirt
momentarily
fired with light.

XX
after Vallejo
Help me
keep the heat
turned up in the
oven of my heart.

The Angelus Bells

I am forever intrigued
by the chorus of four or five
honey-bees pealing the bells
of every foxglove in the hedgerow;

by the elegance of satined leaves
unfolding out of winter gloves,
their veined solar panels
full of focus and certainty;

by the Easter sun rollicking
across cow-splattered fields,
showing off the shy lichen
whitewashing on stone walls;

by an incontinence of dandelions
dribbling along the roads;
by buttercups overflowing
on south-facing ditches;

by the unchoreographed dance
of those bees stuffing the satchels
strapped to their thighs
with this most blessed sweetness.

Freedom

after Seán Ó Ríordáin

Oh of course at times I do envy
them their rites and their rituals,
their casual acceptance,
the unquestioning listening.
But I could never go back down,
down amongst these people,
the bridled, the copied, the second-
hand opinions would strangle me.
I would rail against the rules,
the laws, the peopled temples,
the self-appointed abbots of conscience,
the servility, the cowardice.

Liberty need not howl venomously
across an open prairie of thought;
let me vault the field-gates of religion,
free me from the haggard of opinions,
let me slip the loophole, find reprieve,
let me go face the outback of my fears,
let me admire wind gloriously
galloping across fields of barley;
let the barrel of stars unmercifully
intoxicate me; let me be whacked
by the smudged thumbprint of rainbow,
November sky's ultimate signature.

Laying Bare

A lawnful of light slouched
towards the trembling trees,
soaked, siphoned away by
the leaves lacy underwear,
leaving the garden bloated,
the darkness full of itself
until the kite-moon floated
its bloated bubble of light;
sheets of intimacy flapped,
flagged, defined the line;
the pole stood guard,
the cat picked its steps,
the clouds ran for cover,
a star stationary, maybe alive.

The laying-bare brought
not shock but welcome relief;
picked, pitched in the open,
a man on the face of the earth,
ill at ease in footsteps he
too willingly follows, only now
sees himself for that solitary second
washed smoothly rounded,
a stone on the beach of time,
bereft, washed up, windfall
weeks worn out to nothing,
batting, battling, the breaths,
the plum-days all but plucked,
jam-packed in the jar of the heart.

The President's Prize

So, what's the story?

The pair of limes combing
their heads in the hardy wind,

a shoal of sycamore leaves
shooting across the fairway,

light stripping sheer
flimsy negligees of rain,

poplars slopping and mopping
with their moon-faced leaves,

a carnage of varicose twigs
desecrating the fifteenth green,

a spinney of saplings
springing with sheer delight,

umbrellas snapping and yelping
in triumphant distraction,

the blistering of haws
bursting on bushes,

waterhens scurrying
with their arses in the air,

a pair of black-crows
sitting on their wings,

the bursting of fuchsia bells,
blobs of purple puce,

the freckles of autumn
arriving en-masse,

the wind-washed sky
all demure and azure.

This litany of glory.

Gnostic Psalms

I. Electrical Installation

It was only today when you asked
about the core of the earth wire

did I realise the importance
of being so securely earthed.

II. The Master Tradesman

The darkness does
a great favour
in covering over
the boundary lines
and the flotsam rafts
on various rivers

and showing off in
its vaulted gallery
the master tradesman's
pebble-dashing
scarfed with that
wild splash of scudding.

III. Prayer
after Adam Zagajewski

Forget the high bright flames,
they have never been enough;
God let us be astonished
by the quiet music of love.

IV. Marvel

Reading brought me a long way, slowed me down
to where I could intently listen to the stillness;
hear tautness tickling an unplucked string;
the softness of mist settling on blades of grass;
the swing of his sledge stored in cold stone.

But it was and could never be enough;
it was only when I could sink deeper to where
the music inherent in stillness had the space
to blossom and bloom, that the cavern could resound,
and there was nothing more than to marvel.

V. God

I love the way people who
say they do not believe in God
are always talking about God
and those who say they are atheists
are always making sure you know
that they know there is no God
and those who believe in God
can sicken you with preaching
about what they think is God
whereas the few who know God,
who have been touched by God,
feel no need to say anything.

VI. Last Night
after Antonio Machado

Last night a spring
unleashed delicious water,

quenching my thirsty heart.
Last night a bee-hive
burst open sweet honey
to gladden my aching heart.

Last night the sun rose
with all its mighty warmth
to lighten up my heart.

Last night God itself
in all its resplendence
was alive in my heart.

VII. Knowledge
after Tadeusz Rozewicz

Time will heal everything,
the wounds leave no scar,
grasses cover the graves;
the dead will not rise again.
The world will come to an end;
poetry cannot change that fact.

But the mound of ignorance
can be levelled, the seekers rewarded,
words of wisdom can point the way
to what there was before fire and time;
to what sits patiently within the heart.

VIII. The Well of Myself
after Fernando Pessoa

Stooping over the well of myself
looking down, looking in,
is to come face to face

with something teeming,
a fullness stretching every pore;
a stillness roundly pouring,
its presence pealing, ringing;
a safety, a port, a harbour.

IX. Treasurer
after Jorge Guillen

When he feels the value
of every breath, every moment,
then surely the weeks and years
will look after themselves.

X. Sisyphus

There was no hill,
there never was a hill.
It's just that every morning
when the sun rolls up
we get another chance
to awaken from the fog
of forgetfulness,
roll up our sleeves,
get down to work,
renew our efforts all over,
so that today will be the day
we will not again forget,
that we will be thankful,
appreciate, feel gratitude.

XI. Currency

My flip-side is God,
who, smoothly as a coin
slipped under my tongue,
drew my every breath;
giving life to this body,
giving doubt the slip,
giving me purchase, grip,
down the slope to death.

XII. Copernicus

What mattered most,
in the face of all the
garbed and garbled words,
was that he followed through;
that he knew what stood
at the heart of his world.

XIII. Listen my Friends
after Mirabai

If we could reach him
through immersion in water
I'd have been born as a fish.

If we could reach him
through eating nuts and berries
I'd have been born a monkey.

If we could reach him
through munching leaves,
surely I'd have come as a goat.

If worship of stone statues
could bring us all the way,
I'd adore a granite mountain.

Listen, my friends, this road
is the heart opening, opening,
kissing his feet; joy all night.

XIV. What Matters Most

What matters most is not so much
how this blue ball of earth,
suspended in endless space,
is hurtling around the sun
at some enormous speed,
killing all notions of permanency,

or how the river cascades
down year after year, taking
friends to early graves, taking
loved ones to far-flung places,
its slow march of certainty
taking everything in its path

but that I can stop off into
a space of light that shyly floods
out the plains of myself with
a recognition, a love,
an untouchable knowledge
that is so undeniably there.

XV. Homeward Journey

His handful of years is being ransacked
with a slow yet deadly intent,
exposing what he considered a career
as just months, years, all gone, spent;
the vultures in their pinstripe suits
are making another killing on stock;
the sirens are reaching him from the web,
having lost none of their cheap allure;
he is trawling his treasure trove
through waters he can just about endure.

Only when he sits into the stillness,
follows his breath beneath the foam,
can he feel that outcrop of rock,
that solid island he knows is home.

II

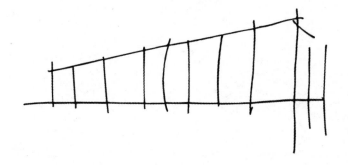

Occupational Therapy

There's no doubt about it;
in a college somewhere
a kid is in training
to be an occupational therapist;
she's my daughter's age,
on the phone to her folks,
worried sick about her Finals
but planning a year out to see Asia
with the new boyfriend.

Little does she know
that I am in training too
for when she comes back,
gets married, settles down;
she will assess me for
the house adaptation grant;
my list of qualifications will include
coronary heart disease,
irritable bowel syndrome
and of course, that old
chestnut, hypertension.

The Old Adversaries

The thought of the approach shot jangles echoes of terror:
can the rescue club carry the water hazard;
could the menacing claws of the Sitka spruce pluck
the ball out of its perfect trajectory and flick it out
behind the line of white stakes. So much depends
on a bad lie, an unlucky bounce or too much loft.

The caddies murmur assurance as yardage is cross-checked,
the right club is finally whipped out of the bag
and given a last wipe across the back of the pants.
They stand apart, silent, alone with themselves,
taking in slow deep breaths, relaxing shoulders and arms,
delaying that extra minute, waiting for the wind to settle.

The battle between trust and doubt rages in the pits
of their stomachs; the swing, the whack, the ping of contact,
a fillet of sod leaving the perfect fairway divot;
their eyes flitting between the ball hanging in its loop,
its utterly helpless lull, and the flag fluttering carelessly;
a benediction of light and wind flecked with spats of rain.

Blithering
across the Tiles

The teardrops streeling
down the cold cheeks
of the windowpanes
know that I love you.

The pianist fingers
of nervous leaves
twitching in the breeze
are playing I love you.

The tree scribbling
on the corrugated roof
of the garden shed
is signing off I love you.

The rain showering,
blithering across the tiles,
blind to the rhythm of itself,
is dancing to I love you.

The wind patiently
fine-tuning its speed
through the tall trees
is reciting I love you.

The long loose
swoosh of swallows,

swooping on flies,
is scrawling out I love you.

The embroidery of stars,
stitching its sequins
to the screen of night,
is deciphering that I love you.

French Kissing

I'd only ever heard of French kissing
and knew nothing of its significance;
so when this girl whose name
I barely knew pushed her tongue
into my mouth outside a dance
hall in Dundrum in the early hours
of a Saturday morning all those years ago
I'd no idea what she was saying.

Sunday Night in Golden

The crowds pushed in ordering drink,
empty glasses raised, time pushing on;
strong men with red faces and broad hands
that could well whip a hurley,
bowing their heads for the first mouthful.

She sucked on a cigarette, blew smoke
up past her eyes, out of the way;
her hair, dyed a light brown,
fuzzed up on top of her head,
undecided if it might be a fashion.

Her high-heeled shoes felt the beat
of the music in the concrete floor,
her jeans creased the outline of panties,
her breasts stood dangerously firm
behind the screen of a blouse.

A squall of laughter broke in a knot
from the corner of her mouth as she
tossed ash all over the floor;
she poured another big bottle,
darted glances across at the neighbours.

Their hands reached for pint glasses,
jokes broke and laughter rose;
they saw her from the corners of their eyes,
throwing her nods of recognition
but very few words of salute.

They could speak with an eye and answer
with a nod; asking all of the questions
with a look, a laugh, a passed drink -
knowing all of the answer in the slapped knee,
the loud laugh, the quick glance, the steady stare.

Pearls

after Rainer Maria Rilke
for Gillian

You are
the string
and the clasp,

without you
the pearls
would roll
and scatter.

Touching

When I am a breeze
I touch your skin

When I am an apple
I taste your mouth

When I am water
I thirst for your tongue

When I am gold
I roll on your finger

When I am the moon
I light up your night

When I am the tide
I come back for you

When I am sunlight
I shadow your breasts

When I am fire
I glow in your eyes

When I am a kiss
I stick on your lips

When I am love
I touch your heart.

Coming Back
from Inishbofin

That evening coming back
from 'Bofin we stood leaning
against the rail, feeling
the thrust of the sea through
the palms of our hands, our boots
gripping the floor of the boat,
our knees lithe and loose,
our bodies trusting the rhythm.

Watching, watching the sea
cavorting, conducting its dance,
its aimless, tireless response,
breakers lost in themselves,
laughter thrown to the wind,
murmurs of immensity rippled,
a ceasefire of sorts agreed,
granting us safe passage.

Back to Cleggan and to Clifden
where music spilled out of a pub,
pulled us in to watch its surge,
rising and rising with no relief,
stranding the guitarist on the stage,
sweeping the fiddler onto the bar;
my meejums keeping pace with your pints,
father and daughters, in tune, again.

Evening in Bath

for Sarah

That July evening in Bath,
stepping out of a café
onto the narrow footpath,
a breeze restless, rustling.

And then stepping back against
the patient softness of a blue
door, letting them pass,
a couple holding hands,

in step, laughing together,
unaware of anything
other than themselves,
lost in their little bubble.

It stalled, stranded something in me.
Was that it, was that all over,
was that part of my life
gone, done away with?

Their bubble of hope blindly
pushing off out into the rapids,
the white-water rapids of love,
to swirl, to twirl, to dance;

to be carried away, swept off
to something new, unknown,
lost in the moment, in the now,

to beach, to berth, to land.
My daughter, excited from the baths,
calls and we walk together
back the narrow streets
to catch the train to Bristol.

Transformation

The transformation was unreal –
the way the scattering of metal filings
on a sheet of paper suddenly
swivelled, turned, surged
to the pull of the magnet.

It was no different that day
minutes after you were born,
standing at the incubator,
first the faint hints of a pull,
then a loosening, an unfettering,
a collapsing into something new,
something different, broader,
barriers breached, swept away,
horizons suddenly stretching;
a giving and a giving way,
this tidal wave of love
charging, surging, engulfing.

Breakfast in London

for Orlaith

That's it, that's what caught my eye:
the way she let him think
that he was choosing the seat!
The café was not very busy;
there were plenty of empty seats;
but there was something in her walk,
a confident pose, almost striding,
and then that little pause,
when she knew;
letting him choose what she already had chosen.

I was finishing a leisurely late breakfast,
just down from the Tate Modern.
It was a sunny Sunday morning;
the light bouncing off the Millennium Bridge
was rough on the eyes
as I came across from St. Paul's.
The Thames churning wide and wonderful,
its banks crowded with architecture;
the thermal mass of polished stone radiating;
the new Shard's glass towering, overlooking,
guarding, reflecting, deflecting light.

They sat across from me;
both in their early thirties,
he with his back to me, dark blue jumper,
unshaven, tousled hair,
both hands resting on the table.

She in a long black dress,
a light silky blue scarf draped for effect.
She sat with her legs splayed apart, black tights.
Then crossing her legs, her hands moving, talking;
both palms up on the table;
opening and closing her fingers, flicking,
releasing, letting butterflies fly, touching his hands;
sitting straight upright.
Did she work in the City;
in law, wear a pinstripe by day?
Was he in theatre, bringing her to see
the new Bacon exhibition?

His thank you, his soft accent.
The notes and the coins offered.
Her hair tossing on her shoulders.
A shadow moved and the sun,
lifting off a tabletop, caught the cut of her chin;
her father's face.
And you knew.
Her shoulders back, her back straight;
her feet firmly on the floor.
He crouched over, elbows on the table;
she opening space, open to the space;
he holding down, restraining, retaining.
And you knew what they did not,
and could not know.

In weeks, months.
People coming together,
a settling into a knowledge
of each other that's blinded until,

and if, the in-love can settle down,
broaden out into love.
A vast complex filtering system,
getting shaken, tossed;
what grains of love would pass through
this milling, this churning, this chaffing.
And you knew, that he, someday,
in a café or sitting room,
or in some departure lounge,
would be crouching further forward;
his face, his face in his hands.

She would outgrow him.
You knew; somehow you knew.

Invitation

for Arthur Broomfield

Come, come, leave Semple Stadium,
leave the Boherlahan-Duallas,
the Moycarkey-Borrises, the Carrick Davinses
and the Clonoulty Rossmores;
leave the guttural roars of that crowd,
their r's rolled sourly and dourly,
like barrels turning on a tarred road,
accents suited to herding cattle,
to scutter plopping on narrow lanes,
to milking parlours and silage pits,
to wet fields and small paddocks
in the shadow of the Galtee Mountains.

And come with me on the train from Brisbane
and be uplifted by the Australian lilt,
like rinsed gravel sparkling off a shovel,
its sing-song sun-filled sound of dry fields,
of tall trees, bark crackling, peeling;
of the kookaburra's waking call,
the sparkling red, blue and tangerine feathers,
the sounds lilting, lifting, clearing,
with space to dip and dive and boom;
come to Taringa and to Toowong,
Toowoomba, Indooroopilly, Corinda,
Woolloongabba and back to Yeerongpilly.

Togged out in Ridiculous White

after Rembrandt's 'Night Watch'

I got there only just in time
to see what was causing all the fuss,
you can see my sad little eyes
still lost in my nights with her;
the gombeen men all agitated,
the women running, cowering;
that yoke with the black hat,
accusations dripping off his pointed nose,
chawing my ear with some shite,
cutting the snot off me with that stare,
his hand extended, the soft palm
of a blessing, was he a priest;
and the old farmer, in from the bog,
dementedly thumping on his drum.

The jumped-up little emperor,
togged out in ridiculous white;
for heaven's sake, what was going on?
Nothing, it seems, a bloody woman,
he wanted to impress a woman,
and this is how he went about it;
no culture, no class, no finesse,
an old-fashioned show of plumage
and a few swords flashing in the night.
Who'd fall for such a dirty scoundrel,
small and stocky, a squire of a thing,
his friends a cabal of cowards?
What woman worth her salt
would roll for him in the morning?

Rhode Island Reds

You do not expect a young man
boarding the metro in Barcelona,
with his quiff of black hair
pulled back in a cow's lick,
a pair of tight black jeans,
tattoos on his bitten fingers
and polished pointed shoes,
to be carrying in his hand
a small cardboard box
punctured with holes;

the high-pitched chirping
of a dozen day-old chicks.
Are they Sussex, I wonder,
with their matronly grey scarf,
or Leghorn in starched white?
Could they be mother's favourite,
the Rhode Island Reds
that scratched, pecked, laid out,
doused in copious dust;
that broke into father's cabbage patch?

But you know by how he sits,
a flat, bored-looking slouch,
that he will never see the pullet's
red comb fresh and full,
its quizzical eye staring,
blinking behind its milky veil;
that he will never feel the
excitement of the first egg,
the small freckled orb of life;
feel it wobbling in the egg cup.

At the Corner of Urgell and Gran Via

Earlier that evening I stood looking
at the old bullring at La Monumental,
the soft low light blanching the brickwork,
picking out the pointing, long flat bricks,
with soldier courses standing over doorways,
walls worn, crumbling, receding,
and knew that brickies back then
had climbed down off scaffolding of a balmy
May evening like this, to drink and tease,
to listen carefully, detect love's rumblings,
tune into a prayer for the soft rains
of love to come, to shower, to douse.

Later, at the corner of Urgell and Gran Via,
your heels crimping wedges of light,
you knotted with anger and confusion,
ready to demolish everything and anything
you thought somehow could tie you down,
the wild savannahs of your fear slashing
any and all ties. Friendship was something
you could only allow to be built through
hours coursing across the pools of your eyes,
slowly testing a foundation of trust,
so that your tears of loss and pain
could well, and slowly spill down your face.

The Cattle Dealer's Daughter

When he let them
mount the stairs
and enter her room
in their tan boots
splattered with cowshit
he had cut some deal.

Sister's Bedroom

What did it take when the cold cold
winds pulled through the tall trees,
lawns bristled with tufted frost
and long corridors glistened in moonlight?
No talking in bed here, no warm
back to cuddle or cold feet to kick;
a wilted St Brigid's cross over the door,
a wash-hand basin standing in the corner;
her school books stacked on the table,
daffodils in a jam-jar on the window board
overlooking the gravelled driveway;
black-and-white photographs of her parents,
an old suitcase, in memoriam cards,
rosary beads at the end of the bed.
It took more than statues dancing
to flickering candles and whitethorn
bursting rapturous for May processions
to find her feet, to hold her steady.

Orpheus

These days when you see him down in Starbucks
you can tell, just by the cut of him,
the glazed suit, the dull shoes, the open-necked shirt,
the tossed hair, the bitten fingernails,
that no matter what they said at the time,
and no matter what brochures he spreads,
no matter how the iPhone bleeps and throbs,
and how he gabbles away about percentages and yields,

that he never ever had what it took:
the trust, the deadly focus, the drive.
His head heavy with the sludge of porn,
he took the easy option, the lazy bastard;
he couldn't push on, pull himself together,
didn't battle, fight, get it over the line,
he ducked and dived, dithered, second-guessed.
He couldn't wait, couldn't trust; he looked back.

The Unfaithful Man

La Casada Infiel
Federico Garcia Lorca

Yes I knew, of course I knew
he was betrothed, shackled, married,
that evening I met him at the river
outside my dreary little town;
the Indian summer was slipping,
the evening draped a dampness,
a pause, a questioning shiver
on our deceitful daring date.
The cut stone of the race
corralled the water into spate;
chestnut's grotesque gourds
shelled out brown conkers;
a dog was barking, a warning,
somewhere across the river.

The touch, the heat of his hand,
pushing me back against the wall,
I wolfed down French kisses
that drenched my parched pussy;
his fingers on the back of my bra
fumbling, finding the clasp,
the haws of my tits shone
taut, taunting his tongue.
the stone chiselling my arse,
the stallion, the mullion of him,
a jabbering javelin of juice;

he was going ballistic, bonkers;
the corbels, the chamfers, the quoins,
a hardy man of stone and verse.

I matched him stride for stride
as he galloped, gulped his passion,
except when I caught sight
of the wedding ring on his finger;
that nearly ruined my night.
I behaved like what I am,
greedy, selfish, a whore,
the daughter wreaking revenge.
Could he be man enough
to take my feast of pleasure
and not fall to pieces in love,
the unfaithful married man
having his bit on the side,
that evening down by the river?

Rent Asunder

after Tibullus
Elegy 1:5

I spun like a top whipped across the floor,
spinning so furiously I rushed the step at the door,
whack-landed on my backside out in the yard;
I hate to admit it, I took it real hard.
It was something being rent asunder,
a breaking down, a sudden going under,
rafters and joists crushing in the jaws of a Hymac,
dust and dirt, nails snapping with a smack;
the dentist levering on a tooth, a molar,
roots snapping, face drained of colour.
Or a tree swinging wildly in a gale wind,
roots slipping out of the grey marl, a blind
fear grappling, puncturing, an own goal,
a heaving wavering, sucking at the sloppy hole,
then crashing, flattening, flaccid, a stain,
the rushing in of light, the gasp of pain.

Besmirched I was by your face, your eyes,
your teeth, your lips telling brazen lies;
your mouth, oh the taste of fags off your kiss,
the sharp smack that I already miss.
You had met some man in a local bar
who whisked you off in his souped-up car
to taverns of music and jokes and song,
to beds of drunken sex all night long.
You loved yourself; it was all about you,
your loss, your pain, and what I could do.

My head was wrecked from this affair;
my heart seemed pulled beyond repair.
I had a life, a family I could not surrender,
in the end I was glad to delete your number.
The grass will grow, the sun shine; my heart
will mend; this indeed has to be a new start.

The Hepworth, Wakefield

David Chipperfield's
bunker of bare concrete
banked on the river
in this West Yorkshire town
stuns and arrests the eye with
its smooth pigmented concrete,
its clean lines and impeccable font,
recessed lighting and
unique shadow lines.
The mass of the huge structure
is ingeniously broken down
into ten trapezoidal blocks
with floor-length windows
looking down onto the river.

But what caught my eye
(beside the fisherman's son
asleep on a little island
in the middle of the river)
was the build of a woman
walking out of the café
on the ground floor level,
thirty-five or thereabouts,
white jeans, pump heels,
hair loosely tied back;
her superbly sculpted breasts
proudly announced
to all and sundry that she
was enjoying a great sex life.

The Man from Porlock

Now you know why I called,
yeah, I was his dealer,
I was collecting my debts.
Surely you knew that already?
And what did I listen to?
The rantings and ravings of a lunatic
that went on for a bloody hour,
and how brave he was, brandishing
a branch when chased by a cow;
a cow never chased anything
in its life for God's sake;
and a big drawn-out yarn
about a crowd up in Grasmere,
wherever the hell that is;
brother and sister in some dungeon
of a cottage, sounded terribly dodgy,
and off he went again raving,
no mention of money mind you,
only all William this and William that,
getting locked in some Tavern
reposing on the banks of the Wye,
and skating across the lakes
with shadows slipping off the fells,
or was that ink dripping off quills,
climbing cat bells, for God's sake;
and not a sign of a shilling
after I traipsing all the bloody way
across the country from Porlock.

The Preparation for Battle

The Iliad, Book 3

First onto the teebox this morning
we welcome Paris, the champion from Troy,
winner not only of the last two majors
but also, it appears, the heart of Helen,
tall and blonde, the prettiest of the WAGs;
his brother Hector is carrying his bag,
emblazoned as usual by the swoosh of Nike.
Look at Paris, the huge driver in his hand,
see the silver studs stiffening the shaft,
see the powerful head, close-cropped,
the lean muscular body, torqueing,
twisting as he loosens up on the tee-box.
The driver twitching like a rod,
snatching, snapping, whipped by wrists
as strong and pliable as any ash sapling.
And here as he sets up, first to drive,
the grip, the stance, the left leg planted,
the fulcrum, the pivot, the slow take-back,
the hips rotating; that all-too-familiar
minute pause at the top of the backswing,
now the drive down, the follow-through,
shoulders, hips and legs all rotating
in one effortless motion of power and timing.
The ball climbing, describing the perfect
orbit, the perfect sine wave,
carrying the bunkers by some distance
dancing along the plush fairway,
the honeymoon shot, opening up the green.

Also onto the teebox we welcome Menelaus,
the warrior fighter all the way from Achaen,
his red hair flaming in its ponytail,
eyes narrowed in their menacing style,
the tension mounting, a wild excitement
surging through the crowds lining the fairways.
The flamboyant Menelaus, the underdog, the chal-
lenger;
see the glaze in those eyes, the cut of his chin,
hoping the gods are on his side this time.
The glove on his right hand well worn;
the unfazed coldness of that steady gaze;
he's here today to trump, to triumph,
settling the ball on its tee, standing
behind it, the club hovering, shivering.
A breeze tugging at the cutthroat pleat
straight down the back of his trousers,
glutes tight, bullsack hanging idle;
leaves jostling for a better view; a stillness
gathering in the shine on his shoes.
His feet shuffling; settling, crouching,
his T-shirt stretched tight across the barrel
of his back catching the sheen of the sun.
Then the ball is gone away out to the left,
his familiar little draw, and slowly, surely,
pulling back right, carrying the sand traps,
shaped perfectly, coming back around
the pair of huge lime trees, using the dogleg,
stalking the centre of the fairway.

The battle has indeed begun.

III

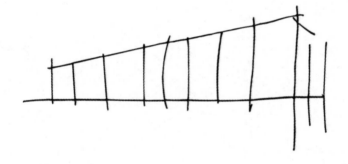

Grennan Lane Walks

I
A battalion of bulls belching,
nostrils flaring, blowing breaths,
pulling, ripping, the short grass;

the nervous choreography
of a wagtail chasing flies
dancing across the lane;

the chaotic choir of blackbirds
thrashing through a bush,
a blaze of communion whites;

a pigeon flapping, stalling,
then gliding out,
a long loose parabola of air;

a bumblebee boringly busy,
undazzled by the saintly blues
of vetch and bluebell;

rows and rows of furrows
creasing the brow of the hill,
streaming down to the river;

the corrugated roof of the empty
barn reverberating to the tune
of a passing shower.

And what will have been harvested
when the stubble, shorn and bare,
lies nurturing the clay in winter's frosts?

II
So, this is as good as it gets then,
for the huddle of young bulls
lying out in the June breeze,
regurgitating, chewing the cud.
They stand, stretching to a flatback,
tails curled, flexing, flicking flies,
the pendulum of their ballsack dangling;
long thin penises squirting piss;
heavy heads swaying off thick necks;
rough tongues wrapping around tufts of grass.

Then a sudden turning away
to frenzied bouts of head-butting,
and dry mounting, holeless rutting
while a lone black bull lopes
off to the far fence and stands there,
bellowing, roaring, calling
the drystocks' empty lament.
They are the dumbest of dumb animals,
prisoners paralysed, content to parade
within the tick-tick of a wire earthing.

Do they not hear, notice the mower
across the road up and down the field,
silage squelched between buttressed walls
sweltering and sweating, leaching and
leaking a trickle of black blood.

Do they yearn, do they long for anything?
To tease, to mount the in-heat heifers?
Are they content in their stolid stupidity?
Does the cow daisy standing on stilts
outside the wire blankly gazing at the sun
not remind them of something or other?
So this is as good as it gets for them then;
settled, satisfied in their discontent,
adding poundage heedless of the trailer
always at the ready in the farmer's yard.

Leavetakings

I
When I see those tiny
liver-coloured blotches
appearing on the back of my hand
I know it's time to finally
settle into the trunk of myself,
feel its immense ballast
securing me against the storms,
sense its roots sinking down
into the reverberating silence,
drawing from its deep well,
allowing the light to bathe,
to soothe, to uplift, to excite.

II
after Osip Mandelstam

Wind fine-combs, pulls
through tangled trees,
composting leaves;

trunks ring out,
counting backwards
into soft white centres;

rough rafters for the roof,
planed planks for the shipwright,
off-cuts for the firewood box;
fisheye knots polished,

secret housings dovetailed,
the joiners finished kitchen;

the choice of finest wood, though,
saved for the coffin-makers.

Over in Japan

For many years now
I have noticed
that every graveyard
I pass I cast
a sweeping glance,
hoping to find
confirmation that there
is actually no more room.

But last night
I read somewhere
that over in Japan
cremation is mandatory;
so it would appear that
even in the complete
absence of graveyards,
people still die.

Flagstone

The guy on the tractor with a
reversible plough will not feel
even the slightest indentation
when he glides through the ground
where the house had stood
for nearly two hundred years.

We had seen the men last week
separating the rubble into a heap,
burning the rotted rafters,
removing the corrugated iron;
and later the loads of topsoil
levelled, and raked of stones.

But you couldn't help but hope
that the flagstone to the front door
is not dumped in some damp ditch.
Facing the road, facing south,
this sandstone store of heat
with the odd sparkle of quartz,

scratched by hobnail boots,
polished by centuries of leather,
the threshold over which the bride
was carried in with excitement,
and, later caused the men to stumble
as they carried out the coffin.

The Day the Train Stopped

i.m. Kieran Meagher

In class all those years ago,
you had argued with deft logic
and a tremendous gush of passion,
that when a fly is hit head-on
by a train, that by the laws
of physics, since the fly very obviously
was stopped in it tracks so to speak,
that the train had stopped too,
for even the minutest millisecond!
I'm sure you never believed the argument;
the laughing eyes were the giveaway.

But when news of your death broke,
time shuddered, stalled in its tracks;
for an unbelievably long minute
we were looking, gaping through a blip,
a chink, rescued from the carousel;
everything picked out with cold edges,
crystallised reliefs peeled from time,
taking us deep down to slow motion,
sealed in, under, underneath the noise;
the silence, the awful realisation
that the train indeed had stopped.

Clear Felling

Before Billie White clear-felled
the wood off Coleman's road,
he applied for a felling licence;
we marked out the boundaries
and the forester assessed the trees.
Then you'd have heard the saw's
pleading insistence,
and the occasional crash
as a top-heavy tree flopped down.

You'd have seen the pyramid of logs
stacked at the side of the road
and the lorries, laden heavy,
rumbling away to the mills.
But, it was still a shock to chance
on the clearing bombed out
with light, only the stubborn
memorial stumps standing,
stranded in a crude symmetry.

So of course it is a shock when
I catch a glimpse over my shoulder
at the clear-felling that happened.
Not just my parents gone but every
single aunt and uncle who stood tall
in my childhood, cleared out;
the uncle cycling to matches,
the one with the finest rhubarb,
clear felled, cleaned out, all gone.

The Barber's Shop in Lincoln Place

I can't believe it when I see my Uncle Bill sitting
in a barber's shop in Lincoln Place in Dublin
having his hair cut by a tall man from Armenia.

His white hair is falling into his lap, he is as usual
picking at his bitten fingernails, even though
a black bib is covering his shoulders and hands.

The barber grimaces, baring his teeth, as some men do,
straining to concentrate through glasses far out on his nose,
his little fingers cocked almost disdainfully.

Bill is sitting still except when the barber from Armenia
moves his head a little to the left or moves it back to the right
so that he can get as close and tidy a haircut as he wants.

I am puzzled of course as to why he is so far from home;
the cottage in Foildearg that his father built, and so
wisely constructed a dummy chimney just for balance.

Is his sister, whom he lives with, still at home, still alive?
And her four children have they all gone to work in England?
It must be well after the year when grandfather was buried.

The barber from Armenia blows the last of the hairs from
around his neck with a hair dryer and is just about to open
the tape at his neck when I catch my eye in the mirror.

Blueprints

i.m. Michael Ryan

I. January

There is no one now
to measure the cock's step
in the January evening;
nor anyone to praise
the shy snowdrops
by the whitewashed wall.

The firm handshake,
the mischievous glint
and the unerring humour
have suddenly disappeared;
our last bastion of defence;
we are bereft, orphaned.

When his body was taken away,
the locker emptied, cleaned out,
there was an absence like nothing before;
the landscape to the cliff-edge
of death suddenly appeared
windswept; completely bare.

II. Tracing

He could trace all round him,
tie up all the family connections;

not only his mother's family,
but every family in the parish,
who had been left a farm by an uncle,
who had married in, and from where.
He could tell you the layout
of the old graveyard in Donohill,
knew the inmates of every plot
almost lost in the high grass.

The other day in the office,
reaching for the tracing paper,
revising the layout of a house,
and this morning driving south,
naming the roads over the motorway,
plotting the geography of Laois;
finding I took in more of him
than I had ever intended;
finding that I carry him
clearer than any blueprint.

III. Seasoning

This January evening I am in Eggenfelden,
about 120 kilometres from Munich,
learning to calculate the heat output
in kilowatt-hours from a kilogram
of well-seasoned beech given the efficiency
of the new generation Brunner stoves,
with their chamotte firelining and
Isaltap sealant cap which can
withstand well over 1,000 degrees of heat

when I see him in the distance of another
January evening, pulling a long limb
of beech off a trailer, standing it up,
then crouching, knees bent, legs
evenly apart; his collarbone testing,
divining the centre of gravity; then the push
forward into the lift; the steady balanced
march across the plot; the stack mounting
at the back of the shed; the seasoning started.

The First Piercing Cut

Of a Saturday morning near Garryglass
surveying boundaries on a Folio map
I noticed a cluster of old buildings
sitting snug in the corner of the holding
and crossing drains and soggy fields
found the lane under a line of beech,
trunks wrapped in jodhpurs of moss;
stone walls whitewashed in algae;
a stone roller backed in against
a hedge, lost in tall nettles; rust
flaking off the rim of a hay-gatherer,
shafts long rotten; apple trees
gone wild sprawling across the haggard,
the cowhouse, brick arched doorways,
the dull heat-trap of limestone.

This could be Doherty's in Donohill,
and you mother, standing, arms folded,
hair black, in that snap from '42;
the long low farmhouse, milk churns
standing stout on the stepped platform,
you lifting, carrying the brimming buckets,
the creamery cart crushing tramlines through
the cobbled yard's dollops of horseshit.
The first piercing cuts, milk pealing
against the inside of the scoured bucket,
your two hands working, stroking the teats,
one after the other in quick tempo,
or the two hands together in unison,
bucket balanced between your knees,
forehead resting against the warm flank.

The Harsh Snap
of a Gate Opening

I
We'd hear you in the kitchen or hear
the door of the shed, your bike crunching
the gravel, the hasp closing the gate,
and you'd be away up the road to Doherty's
or Kelly's of Aileen. The cows, the milking,
the rain, the cow-shit on everything, wellingtons,
aprons and hands, the odd splash into the face,
the older cows heavy and docile, the heifers
kicking, roaring, bellowing for their calves.

II
From the motorway of a Saturday evening,
a bane of Friesians in a long looping line
along a scuttered lane beside a hedge,
the whalehump of the Galtees in the background,
the September leaves losing their grip,
grains of gold gusting on the ground,
the match chat bubbling away on the radio
as if everything was as it always was,
and he'd be waiting with stick in hand

ushering them in, pushing, heaving, hooves
slithering on the concrete, in to the excited
thud-thud-thud heartbeat of the milking machine;
wellingtons, apron, arms bare to the elbows,
washing the engorged udders, checking for mastitis,

the bottle of brown medication on a dusty shelf;
walking up and down the pit, hands clasped
behind his back, whistling snatches of songs;
then the harsh snap of a gate opening.

III
When the second parent dies, the hub
is knocked clean out of the wheel,
the spokes spring lose, the rim buckles.
The orchard of grief is forever littered
with the windfalls of pain. We go on,
strong in our abandonment but always
a gate loose, on the latch, ready to swing
wide open, and the crushing heaving loss
rushes in to engulf, to engorge, to swamp.

Working the Blower

In Memory of Her

I. Keeping the Fire Going

The Wild Colonial Boy
was from the County of Armagh
those Sunday mornings;
the tablecloth caught a pane
of sunlight and bounced it
back across the kitchen.
Cats waited at the open door;
light crept across the floor
to the foot of the stairs
where father hung the mirror;
her hair in a bun, her bib
tight at the waist, she worked
the blower with its dreaded belt,
keeping the fire going.

II. Plaiting her Hair

The light slanting through the window
onto the side of her face
would have enthralled Vermeer,
her mouth ever so slightly lopsided,
something you'd only notice in the mirror.
Her thin white hair, pulling the brush
through it, one side then the other
down over the front of her shoulders

in slow absent-minded strokes.
She plaits the hair, breaking it evenly
into three strands, combing it out,
trimming the broken ends,
starting from the poll of her neck,
bringing one from the left, one from the right,
working out to the end, then twisting it
up into a bun on the back of her head,
clipping it, pinning it into place.

The Vacant Plots

I. Walking on the Moon

The night before they walked on the moon,
an endlessly bright Saturday night,
Denis Byrnes sat in our yard,
his hair sigh-falling onto the gravel,
father giving him a short back and sides,
mother giving him one of Myles's shirts.
He sat there staring across the yard
at the bicycles resting against the hedge,
listening to the crows squabbling, settling in
the sycamores up near Horgan's;
gazing out at the Galtees all summer flushed;
at the herringbone clouds soaked in colour.
Looking as blank as any kid could look
the night before his father's funeral.

II. Bacon

The pale mottled marble counter,
the balance scales, the lump weights,
reaching down into that deep tub,
brine dripping, cavities of salt,
slow cured, steeped, saturated,
the scalded skin, light, hairless;
my fingers burning at the touch.

III. Christmas Morning

Later, books on the table,
the others stomping on the gravel
as they came in from Mass,
walking back roads paved
with glistening palms of ice;
the shapes of familiar trees,
looking across empty fields,
the tufts of grass cocking
their white caps of frost;
the sun playing hide and seek
on the hills above Cappawhite;
the trees with frostbitten wrists
and heron shins standing sentry,
their roots sunk deep beyond it all.

IV. Ciotóg

I miss the way,
being left-handed,
he would get confused
and annoyed,
not knowing
if he was loosening
or tightening a bolt.

V. My Brother Cutting Grass

Why am I so bothered
to see him, sleeves up,
farmer's tan, a red can
of petrol, this July evening,
mowing the vacant plots?

Curriculum Vitae

after Wislawa Szymborska

We all know this résumé will be shredded
so best keep it short and sweet;
there is no need for the passport photograph;
no one is really bothered about appearances.
Nor is there any reference to aspirations
to someday playing off single figures;
nor indeed is there any explanation
as to why our Labrador is named after Beckett.

All you need to know about me is this:
by and large I've managed to shy away from greed,
and I seem to have a weakness for kindness,
which I know I inherited from my mother.
I think it is OK not to get drunk.
On the whole it's fine to be content;
but what does the business above all else
is this knowing, this knowing that I am loved.

The Pin

It looked nothing, the old steel pin
with a crooked point always standing
in the shed at the cottage in Lisheen.
It was a two-foot piece of prong
from a horse-drawn hay-gatherer;
one of those high-wheeled contraptions
with an array of curved steel bars
that pulled swathes of hay in towards
the piker in the middle of the meadow,
where with a frightening rattle of gears
and springs and dust it lifted clear;
then with a light toss of the reins,
a jolt on the traces, a push on the collar,
the horse jerked away, leaving the hayseed
perfume floating in the warm air,
the stubble raw and bare; his fork
reaching, scooping, pulling, lifting,
his arms pumping, the pike taking shape,
braces hitching up the loose trousers,
the evening eventually giving way.

In his hands that pin could be anything,
hold a line taut on the potato ridge,
lift a slate, tap out a cotter pin,
tighten strands of wire with a twist,
prise staples from posts, hacking
in with the curved point, then levering,
the staples molar-like grip loosening,

pulled clear, the splayed spikes tapped
into shape and stored in an old tea canister.
Somehow he could not manage to pin down
the years when they started to run wild;
his talk became littered with a litany of the dead;
he just sat back on the couch in the kitchen,
let the liver spots multiply on his hands,
his questions gathering in less of the answers,
slipping, losing, falling, giving up.
Let poetry then be my paperweight,
to pin down the flysheets of memory,
collect the fresh rich haywords,
saved and honed, the poem's taken shape.

The Meadow

after Czelaw Milosz

It's more than enough now
after more than forty years,
to chance on the smell of hay,
for the satchels of memory to burst
and feel again the fork in my hands,
the welts across my palms,
see the swathes bristling,
dust dancing in the sunlight,
hear the guttural accents
arguing about hurling matches,
hear father tracing and teasing,
smell the whiff of the Gold Flakes,
the yellow box in the stubble.

But there is no going back:
that field is poached and pockmarked,
the hedges and ditches overgrown,
the trees cut for firewood;
the matches fought and forgotten,
all of the men dead and buried,
lost to us forever, forever.
This life is not some trial run,
regardless of our misunderstandings.
Can I instead find the courage
to follow the rhythm of my breath,
can I turn within, can I trust,
can I reap the harvest of this meadow?

Storm in Lisheen

She had us cower in a corner of the kitchen,
well away from the windows of the cottage,
when the rough yard-brushes of trees
swayed and swooshed across an immense floor
of sky and the clouds, swollen to a black
bulge, loomed and burst, losing their
load with a beautiful helplessness,
ponding, plopping down into puddles,
inconsolable tears guttering down
the puttied glass of the blinded windows.

Lightning silently ripped the sky apart,
photographing every traneen in the meadow,
catching cows loitering under trees,
reddening wires socketed to walls.
She taught us to slowly count the seconds,
taught us to measure the miles, waiting
for the first whip-cracks to unleash
a collapsing of thunder, like being inside
a tar barrel under the tailgate of a lorry
relieving itself of an avalanche of gravel.

Afterwards, standing outside in the yard,
gutters gurgling a belated commentary,
trees dripping wet, standing naked
and uncertain as lost leaves floated
and puddles gawked nervously at the sun;
the pair of cats unsurprisingly dry,

snootily snatching their paws off the ground;
the sky all washed, hanging out to dry;
across the hedge the sturdy hump of
the Galtees resplendent and undiminished.